Newcastle Elementary School
8440 136th Ave SE
Newcastle, WA 98059

What's **sacred** to me?

Religious Food

Anita Ganeri

RAINTREE
STECK-VAUGHN
PUBLISHERS

A Harcourt Company

Austin   New York
www.steck-vaughn.com

Contents

Published by Raintree Steck-Vaughn Publishers, an imprint of Steck-Vaughn Company

Printed in Italy. Bound in the United States.
1 2 3 4 5 6 7 8 9 0 05 04 03 02 01

Library of Congress Cataloging-in-Publication Data
Ganeri, Anita.
Religious food / Anita Ganeri.
      p.   cm.—(What's sacred to me?)
   Includes bibliographical references and index.
   Summary: Describes the different foods prepared in various religious ceremonies by Hindus, Jews, Muslims, Buddhists, Christians, and Sikhs.
   ISBN 0-7398-2762-6 (hard)
   0-7398-3124-0 (soft)
   1. Food—Religious aspects—Juvenile literature.
   2. Sacred meals—Juvenile literature.
   [1. Food—Religious aspects. 2. Sacred meals. 3. Fasts and feasts.] I. Title.

BL65.F65.G36 2000
291.4'46—dc21   99-059602

Special Food

What is your favorite thing to eat? Is it ice cream, candy, or delicious pizza? Why do you like it so much?

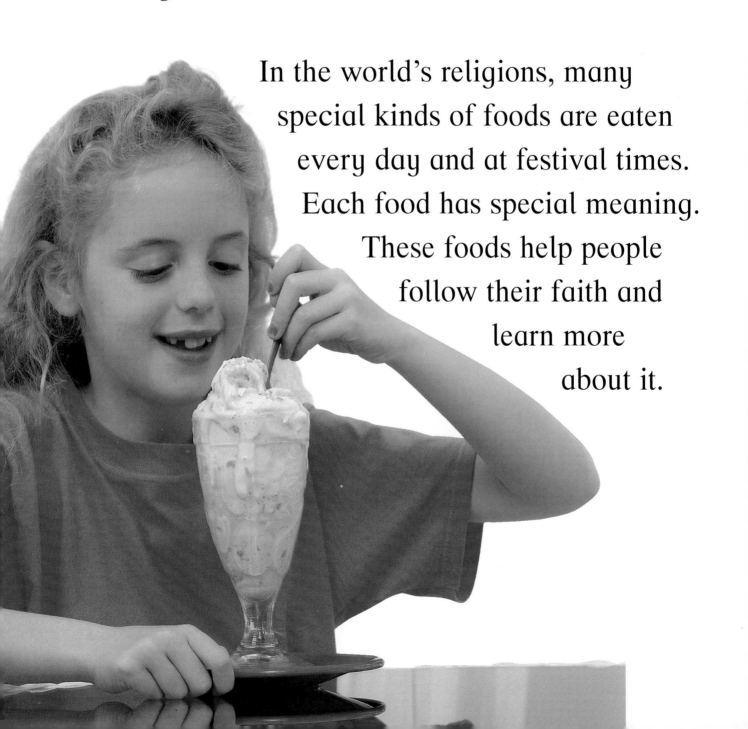

In the world's religions, many special kinds of foods are eaten every day and at festival times. Each food has special meaning. These foods help people follow their faith and learn more about it.

Hindu Offerings

Many Hindus are vegetarians. They believe that all life is **holy**. They do not eat meat because they do not want to kill or harm any animals. Hindus eat their food with their fingers from large plates, called thalis, like the one below.

When Hindus worship, they offer food to God. This can be sweet foods or fruit, like coconuts or bananas. Offerings like these are called **prashad**. Everyone shares the food and receives God's **blessing**.

At a Hindu wedding, the bride and groom sprinkle roasted rice, butter, and grain into a special fire. They believe that the fire carries their offerings up to God. Afterward, there is a great feast.

Sweet foods are made at home or are
bought from stores or stands. At weddings
and festivals, Hindus give gifts of sweets to
friends and relatives. The sweets are made
from milk, nuts, coconut, and sugar.

Jewish Food Laws

On Friday night a Jewish family eats a meal together to celebrate the start of Shabbat. This is the Jewish sabbath. The meal begins with a blessing said over a glass of wine.

This is a loaf of challah, which is specially baked bread for Shabbat. It is made in the shape of a braid. There are always two loaves of challah on the Shabbat table. Everyone in the family has a share.

There are many rules about Jewish food. Food that Jews may eat is called **kosher**. It can be bought from a kosher store. Kosher food includes fruit, vegetables, beef, lamb, and fish. Pork, rabbit, and shellfish are not kosher.

Each of the foods on this plate has a special meaning. The foods are eaten at the festival of **Pesach**, or Passover. They remind people how, long ago, God helped the Jews escape from slavery to freedom.

Buddhist Food Gifts

Buddhist monks are given food by followers who live near their **monastery**. This is called giving **alms**. Giving alms to the monks and nuns is part of a Buddhist's duty.

These monks are having their one meal of the day, which they always eat before midday. Afterward, they can drink water but will go without food until the next day.

On special occasions, such as the Buddha's birthday, people take food, flowers, and **incense** to the monastery. These are offered to a Buddharupa, a statue of the Buddha. Then the food is given to the monks as a gift.

At festival times Buddhists visit the monastery to honor the Buddha and to enjoy a meal together. Many Buddhists do not eat meat because they do not believe in killing or harming animals.

Special Christian Food

At a service that is often called Holy Communion, Christians eat bread and drink wine or grape juice that has been blessed by a priest or minister. This reminds Christians of the last meal that Jesus ate with his friends. It helps them feel closer to him.

This boy is making pancakes to celebrate Shrove Tuesday. (*Shrove* means "forgiven.") This is the day before **Lent**. People use up the rich foods in their homes, such as eggs, butter, and oil. During Lent many Christians give up eating some types of food. They remember how Jesus once spent 40 days **fasting** in the wilderness.

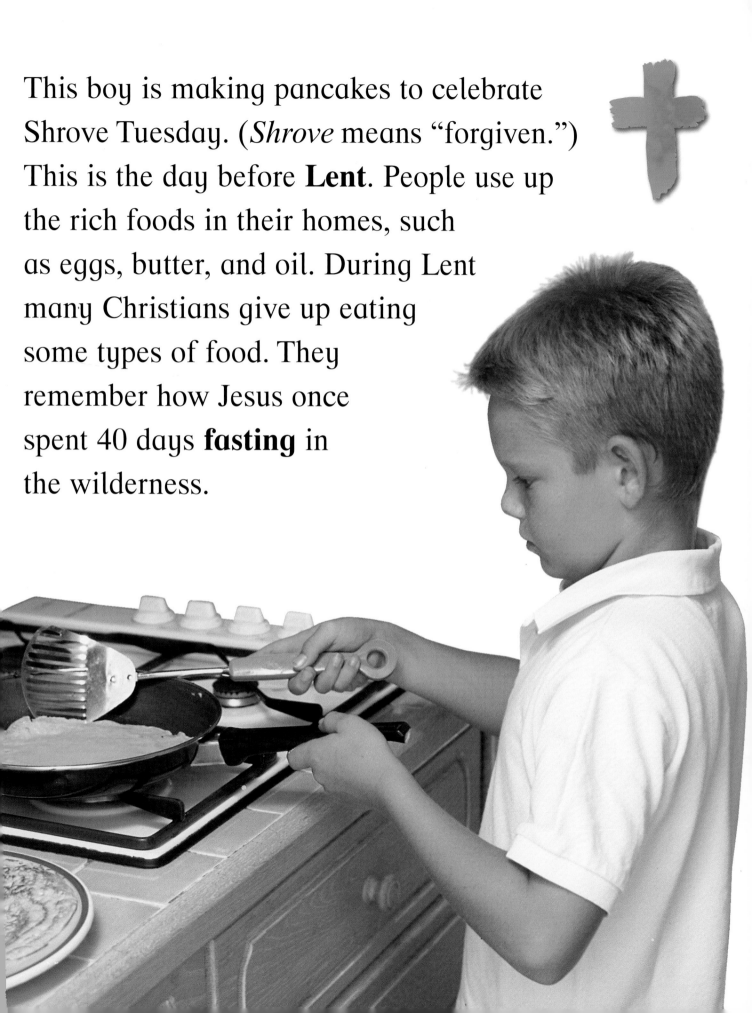

At Easter, Christians eat hot cross buns to remind them of how Jesus died on the cross. They believe that three days later Jesus was resurrected, that is, raised from the dead. Christians eat Easter eggs at Easter to celebrate new life.

This church is decorated with fruit,
vegetables, bread, and flowers to celebrate
the harvest festival. Christians go to a
service in church to say "thank you" for the
harvest and for all God's gifts and goodness.

Muslim Fasts and Feasts

For Muslims, sharing food with guests is an important way of making them welcome. This picture shows Muslims eating a midday meal of chicken, rice, and bread.

Food that Muslims are allowed to eat is
called **halal**. Muslims can buy halal meat,
fruit, and vegetables at special shops like
this one. Muslims are not allowed to eat
pork or to drink alcohol.

 During **Ramadan** Muslims fast from dawn to sunset. This means they have nothing to eat or drink. They do this to obey **Allah**'s wishes. After evening prayers they enjoy a family meal.

These sweet foods and sugared almonds are for the festival of Id ul-Fitr, which marks the end of Ramadan. This happy occasion begins with a great feast. People also exchange gifts and cards.

Sikhs Sharing Food

At the end of all Sikh services, everyone shares a sweet dish called karah prasad, eaten from the same plate. It is prepared in a special way. A prayer is said, and a special sword called a **kirpan** is used to mix the ingredients together.

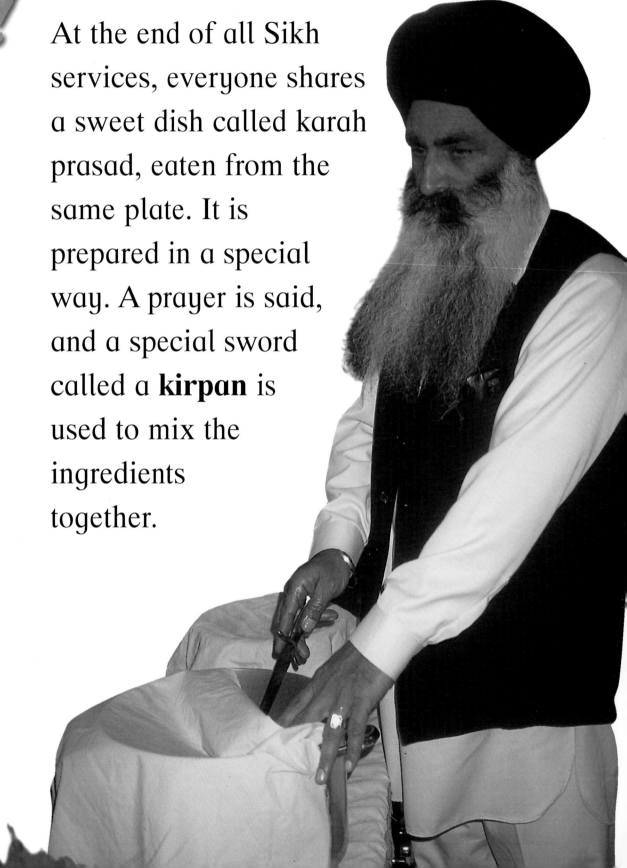

Here karah prasad is being given out at the
end of a Sikh wedding. Sikhs gain strength
from eating and worshiping together.
Sharing food also shows that everyone is
equal in God's eyes.

The end of a service is usually followed by a shared meal in the **langar**. This is the name for the **gurdwara**'s kitchen and all the food cooked in it. The meal is served to all the worshipers and is given free to all. Many people help to cook and serve it.

A special ceremony is held at which Sikhs become full members of their religion. They drink a mixture of sugar and water called amrit. It is stirred with a double-edged sword called a **khanda**. Amrit is also sprinkled on their heads and hands.

Find Out More About

Pages 4 & 5 A Hindu meal traditionally consists of several different vegetable dishes, together with rice or bread, such as chapatis. It is served in small separate dishes on a large steel tray called a thali, or on a banana leaf. Most Hindus are vegetarians, although some eat chicken and fish. Hindus do not eat beef. They believe that the cow is sacred because it is linked to the god Krishna, who was brought up by a cowherd and his wife, and because it provides life-sustaining milk and dung for fuel. As part of their culture, Hindus eat with their right hands. The left hand is traditionally associated with "unclean" tasks, such as washing. Prashad is food that is offered to God in a temple or home shrine to be blessed. It is then shared among the worshipers so that everyone shares in God's blessing.

Pages 6 & 7 Food plays an important part in a Hindu wedding. It is used symbolically during the religious ceremony, conducted by a priest around the sacred fire. Apart from sprinkling rice, grains, and ghee (clarified butter) into the sacred fire, the couple shower each other with rice grains that have been blessed by the priest. Hindu weddings can be very lavish. After the religious ceremony, there is a sumptuous feast for the guests. As at all Hindu celebrations and festivals, gift boxes of Indian sweet foods are sent to friends, relatives, and business associates to mark the happy occasion. Each region of India has its own specialty sweet foods.

Pages 8 & 9 On Shabbat the evening family meal begins with a blessing said over wine and two loaves of challah. This is then shared among all those present. There are always two loaves of bread on the table in memory of the time that the Jews spent wandering in the wilderness after the Exodus from Egypt. They had to collect two portions of manna (the food sent to them by God) on the day before Shabbat. They did this because Shabbat was a day of rest, so no gathering of manna could be done. Until it is eaten, the challah is covered with a cloth embroidered with Shabbat symbols such as the plaited challah loaves themselves, a bottle of wine, or the Shabbat candles.

Pages 10 & 11 The laws governing what Jews may or may not eat are written in the Torah, part of the Jewish scripture. Many Jews keep these laws very strictly. All fruit and vegetables may be eaten. Animals with cloven hooves that chew their cuds, such as sheep, goats, cows, and deer are

kosher, but animals that are only one of these things, such as pigs or camels, are not. Most birds are not kosher, apart from ducks, chickens, and turkeys. Fish are only kosher if they have both fins and scales. Shellfish are not permitted. Dairy foods, such as milk and butter, are not eaten at the same time as meat. The foods served at Pesach are part of the ceremony called the Seder. They remind Jews of their ancestors' slavery in Egypt and of their escape. A roasted shankbone represents the sacrifice of the Paschal lamb; bitter herbs, the pain of slavery; a sweet paste of apples, wine, and nuts, called charoset, is for the bricks and mortar the Jewish slaves used to build cities for the Egyptian pharaoh; parsley symbolizes the hope and renewal of spring; a roasted hard-boiled egg, the sacrifices in the ancient Temple; a bowl of salt water, the slaves' tears. Matzah is the unleavened bread, like flat crackers, the Jews baked when they escaped from Egypt and had no time for bread dough to rise. During the eight days of Passover, no leavened food, called chametz, is eaten.

Pages 12 & 13, 14 & 15 For Buddhists a gift or an act of generosity toward a monk or nun is called dana. It is believed to bring the givers merit that will help them in their next lives (Buddhists believe in reincarnation). The most usual gift is that of the midday meal, placed in the monks' alms bowls. Also listed in the sacred texts are clothing, means of transportation, garlands, perfumes, ointment, bedding, dwellings, and lighting. Apart from the gifts they receive from followers, the monks and nuns own very few belongings. When offerings are made in the temple or monastery, food is placed in front of an image of the Buddha as an act of generosity. Many temples also have kitchens where volunteers prepare food for the monks, followers, and other visitors, especially on special days, such as the Buddha's birthday.

Pages 16 & 17 Holy Communion, at which worshipers share bread and wine or grape juice, is an important service in the Christian church. The service is known by many different names such as Mass, the Eucharist, or the Lord's Supper. It reminds Christians of Jesus' words to his disciples as they shared the Last Supper together. He told them that whenever they ate bread or drank wine in the future, they should do so in memory of him. Ordinary bread is sometimes used, but more often there are special round wafers marked with a cross. The bread is consecrated as the "body" of Christ. The wine is consecrated as the "blood" of Christ. Lent is the name for the six weeks before Easter, beginning on Ash Wednesday. It is a time when Christians remember the days Jesus spent in the wilderness. It is also a time for confessing any wrongdoings in order to make a new start at Lent. Traditionally, plain food was eaten during Lent. Pancakes were made before Lent to use up any rich food in the house.

Pages 18 & 19 It is traditional to eat hot cross buns on Good Friday, the day that Jesus was crucified. The cross is a reminder of how Jesus died. The mixture of spices in the dough reminds Christians of the spices that Mary Magdalene and a friend, who visited Jesus' tomb on Sunday, took to anoint his body. They found the tomb empty. Eggs are an ancient symbol of new life. Chocolate eggs are given at Easter to celebrate Christians' belief in Jesus' new life when he rose again from the dead. The breaking of the egg may also suggest the opening of Jesus' empty tomb.

Pages 20 & 21 In Islam, food that is allowed by Allah is called halal. Food that is forbidden by Allah is called haram. These rules are set down in the Koran, the Muslims' holy book. By obeying them, Muslims are obeying Allah's wishes for how they should live their lives. All fruit, vegetables, and fish are halal. Meat, such as lamb, chicken, and beef, is halal but only if it has been killed in a particular way. First, the animal must be dedicated to Allah. Then the animal's throat is cut, and its blood is allowed to flow freely. It becomes unconscious immediately. Muslims are not allowed to eat pork or anything that comes from a pig. Anything cooked with the fat of animals that have not been sacrificed to Allah is also haram. Drinking alcohol is forbidden.

Pages 22 & 23 During the month of Ramadan, Muslims fast from dawn until sunset. This is sawm, one of the Five Pillars of Islam. The purpose of fasting is to obey Allah's wishes, as written in the Koran, and to practice both mental and physical self-discipline and self-control. It also helps Muslims appreciate what it feels like to go hungry. All adult Muslims are obliged to fast. Children under seven do not fast. Older children fast, but not as strictly as adults. People who are ill or physically weak are excused from fasting, as are menstruating or pregnant women. These people are expected to fast at a later date. Tables are published giving the times of sunrise and sunset during Ramadan so that people know when to begin their fasts. At sunset they have a light snack, followed by a main meal after evening prayers.

Pages 24 & 25 & 26 Karah prasad is a sweet, pudding-like food made from flour, sugar, water, and ghee (clarified butter). It is kept in a steel bowl and is shared at the end of all Sikh services and ceremonies. It is food that has been blessed by God and is shared to show that, in God's eyes, everyone is equal. This is a key Sikh belief. The karah prasad is prepared in accordance with the Rahit Maryada, the Sikh code of behavior, by men or women who have bathed and put on clean clothes. As they cook the mixture, they recite verses from the Guru Granth Sahib, the Sikh holy book. During worship the food is placed near the Guru Granth Sahib in the gurdwara. The langar is a communal meal offered to all worshipers and visitors to the gurdwara. The practice was begun by Guru Nanak, the founder of Sikhism. The food is simple and vegetarian. Eating the langar together demonstrates that everyone is equal.

Page 27 Amrit is a nectar made by dissolving sugar crystals in water. It is stirred in a steel bowl using a ceremonial double-edged sword called a khanda. When babies are taken to the gurdwara to be named, they are sometimes given amrit afterward. It is also drunk by Sikhs joining the Khalsa, the Sikh community, and becoming full members of their religion. It is drunk from a shared bowl to show equality. It is also sprinkled on the initiates' eyes and hair. The Khalsa was begun by Guru Gobind Singh in 1699.

Glossary

Allah The Muslim name for God.

alms Gifts of money, food, or clothes.

blessing God's love and care. A blessing is also a short prayer thanking or praising God.

fasting Going without food.

gurdwara A place where Sikhs meet to worship and to learn.

halal Food that Muslims are allowed to eat.

holy To do with God or the gods. It also means someone or something that should be worshiped.

incense Sweet-smelling spices made into a block or stick.

khanda The two-edged sword that symbolizes the Sikh religion.

kirpan A steel dagger or sword worn by Sikhs, often in a smaller size, and used in Sikh ceremonies.

kosher Food that Jewish people are allowed to eat.

langar This means "the anchor" and is a kitchen where the food is prepared.

Lent The 40 weekdays beyween Ash Wednesday and Easter, a time of fasting and repenting for many Christians.

Monastery A place where monks live, work, and worship.

Pesach A Jewish festival that celebrates how the Jews escaped from Egypt thousands of years ago. It is also called Passover.

prashad Food offered to God by Hindus as part of worship.

Ramadan A month in the Muslim calendar when Muslims fast from dawn until sunset.

Books to Read

HINDU

Wood, Angela. *Hindu Mandir.* Milwaukee, WI: Gareth Stevens, 2000.

JEWISH

Miller, Deborah Uchill and Karen Ostrove. *Fins and Scales: A Kosher Tale.* Rockville, MD: Kar-Ben Copies, 1991.

Penny, Sue. *Judaism.* Austin, TX: Raintree Steck-Vaughn, 1997.

BUDDHIST

Ganeri, Anita. *Buddhist* (Beliefs and Cultures). Danbury, CT: Children's Press, 1997.

Quinn, Daniel P. *I Am Buddhist.* New York: Rosen Group, 1996.

CHRISTIAN

Chambers, Catherine. *Easter.* Austin, TX: Raintree Steck-Vaughn, 1998.

Rock, Lois. *The Time of Jesus.* Colorado Springs, CO: Lion Children's Books, 1999.

SIKH

Chambers, Catherine. *Sikh* (Beliefs and Cultures). Danbury, CT: Children's Press, 1997.

GENERAL SERIES ON RELIGION

Beliefs and Cultures series (Children's Press, 1997/8)

Children Just Like Me series (DK Publishing, 1997)

Food and Festivals series (Raintree Steck-Vaughn, 1999)

Picture Acknowledgments: Cephas (J. F. Riviere) 18, (Frank B. Higham) 19, (Nigel Blythe) 20; CIRCA Picture Library (John Smith) 25; Eye Ubiquitous (David Cumming) 6, (Paul Seheult) 18; Chris Fairclough 21, 27; Sally and Richard Greenhill (Sam Greenhill) 4; Robert Harding 8, 10, 11, 14; The Hutchison Library title page, 13, 16; Christine Osborne Pictures 4, 7, 9, 26; Panos Pictures (J. Holmes) 5, (Jean Leo Dugast) 12; Peter Sanders 22, 23; Trip (H Rogers) 15, (H Rogers) 24; Wayland Picture Library 3, 17.

Index

Entries in **bold** are pictures.